ID0929330

ASK
ABOUT

A
S
I
A

Mason Crest Publishers Inc.
370 Reed Road
Broomall, Pennsylvania 19008
(866) MCP-BOOK (toll free)

Copyright © 2003 by Mason Crest Publishers. All rights reserved. No part of this publication may be reproduced or transmitted in any form or by any means, electronic or mechanical, including photocopying, recording, taping, or any information storage and retrieval system, without permission in writing from the publisher.

First printing

1 2 3 4 5 6 7 8 9 10

Library of Congress Cataloging-in-Publication Data on file at the Library of Congress.

ISBN 1-59084-203-0
ISBN 1-59084-198-0 (series)

Printed in Malaysia.

ᒪ T

Adapted from original concept produced by
Vineyard Freepress Pty Ltd, Sydney.
Copyright © 2001 Vineyard Freepress Pty Ltd.

Project Editor: Valerie Hill
Text: Judith Simpson
Design Production: Fisheye Design
Consultants: Joan Grant, Cuong Phu Le, Thuat Van Nguyen
Cartography: Peter Barker
Images: Mike Langford; Travel Indochina; Peter Barker; World Expeditions; St Monica's Primary School, Footscray, Victoria; Denis Buckley; Sue Bliss; Samsam, Pauline Wesselink; Belinda Bennett; Jane Cameron; A.A.Balkema Publishers; AAP; Hoa Trung; Maurice Durand Collection of Vietnamese Art, Yale University; Tony Eardley; United Nations High Commisioner for Refugees.

COVER: Door in the old quarter of Hanoi.

TITLE PAGE: Bamboo percussion musical instrument in a performance in Ho Chi Minh City.

CONTENTS: A long walk to market carrying fresh vegetables in *don ganh*.

INTRODUCTION: Curious and friendly children greet visitors.

Vietnam

MASON CREST PUBLISHERS

j959.7
SIM

CONTENTS

THE LAND

RULERS OF THE LAND

WAR AND INDEPENDENCE

MODERN VIETNAM

DAILY LIFE

INTRODUCTION

Vietnam is a country of great beauty and variety. Many of its people live outside the busy towns and cities, surviving on what food they can obtain from land and sea. Through the ages, the courageous and hard-working Vietnamese have defended their country against some of the largest nations in the world. During the twentieth century, Vietnam was painfully divided by a long war, which left it one of the poorest countries in Asia. Barely twenty-five years have passed since the north and south were officially reunited under a Communist government.

Conditions within Vietnam have been slow to improve, but now links with other countries are helping the economy grow stronger. Today, the Vietnamese are working to blend the old with the new, and to secure a better future for the children through education, the development of modern industries, and friendship with other nations.

THE SHAPE OF VIETNAM

Vietnam lies south of China, curving like a letter "S" along the eastern coast of the Southeast Asian peninsula, with Laos and Cambodia on its western border. Mountains covered in rainforest run down the western side, linking the north with the south. Some of the narrow coastal strip is edged with white, sandy beaches. At Ha Long Bay, mountains spill into the Gulf of Tongking, forming at least 3,000 rounded, limestone islands. More than three-quarters of Vietnam's people live on the flat plains near the coast, or in the river valleys that run between the mountains and hills. A few occupy the high country and the rest crowd into towns and cities.

▲ Water lilies, green rice fields, and misty mountains.

CLIMATE

Vietnam has a tropical monsoonal climate. In the north, temperatures can drop below freezing on winter days when cold winds sweep down from China. The climate further south is hot all year round. From May to October, monsoon winds bring heavy rains and high temperatures to both north and south. Violent winds, called typhoons, strike the central and northern areas during the monsoon season.

▲ Flowers grow easily in the rich soil.

▼ Terraced rice fields make cultivation possible on steep mountain slopes.

VIETNAM
is in the south of the Asian continent. Its name means "People of the South"
People – *Viet*
South – *Nam*
Viet Nam

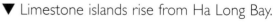
▼ Limestone islands rise from Ha Long Bay.

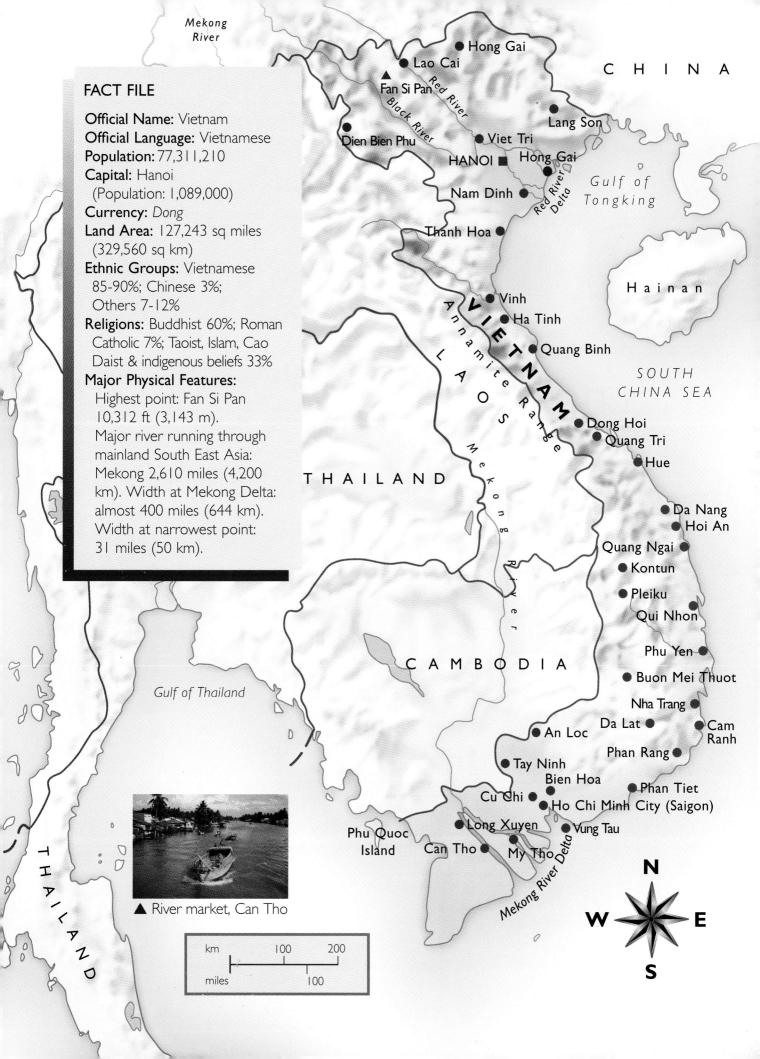

Mekong River

FACT FILE

Official Name: Vietnam
Official Language: Vietnamese
Population: 77,311,210
Capital: Hanoi
(Population: 1,089,000)
Currency: Dong
Land Area: 127,243 sq miles
(329,560 sq km)
Ethnic Groups: Vietnamese
85-90%; Chinese 3%;
Others 7-12%
Religions: Buddhist 60%; Roman
Catholic 7%; Taoist, Islam, Cao
Daist & indigenous beliefs 33%
Major Physical Features:
Highest point: Fan Si Pan
10,312 ft (3,143 m).
Major river running through
mainland South East Asia:
Mekong 2,610 miles (4,200
km). Width at Mekong Delta:
almost 400 miles (644 km).
Width at narrowest point:
31 miles (50 km).

CHINA

Hong Gai
Lao Cai
▲ Fan Si Pan
Red River
Black River
Lang Son
Dien Bien Phu
Viet Tri
HANOI ■ Hong Gai
Nam Dinh
Red River Delta
Gulf of Tongking
Thanh Hoa

Hainan

Vinh
Ha Tinh
Quang Binh
SOUTH CHINA SEA

Annamite Range
VIETNAM
LAOS
Mekong River
Dong Hoi
Quang Tri
Hue

THAILAND

Da Nang
Hoi An
Quang Ngai
Kontun
Pleiku
Qui Nhon

CAMBODIA

Phu Yen
Buon Mei Thuot
Nha Trang

Gulf of Thailand

An Loc
Da Lat
Cam Ranh
Phan Rang
Tay Ninh
Bien Hoa
Cu Chi
Ho Chi Minh City (Saigon)
Phan Tiet
Long Xuyen
Vung Tau
Phu Quoc Island
Can Tho
My Tho
Mekong River Delta

▲ River market, Can Tho

THAILAND

km   100   200
miles   100

N
W   E
S

THE MEKONG RIVER DELTA

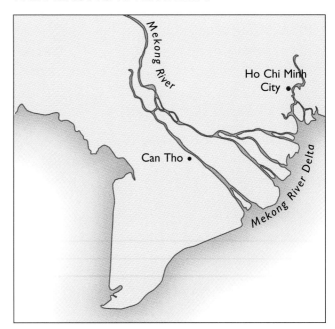

RIVER DELTAS

When a large river nears the sea, it often splits into smaller branches to create a delta of low-lying, well-watered, fertile land. Vietnam is topped and tailed with major river deltas. This is why the Vietnamese liken their country to a *don ganh*—a bamboo pole with a basket hanging from each end.

The northern "basket" is the Red River Delta, where the main river and its tributaries provide water to irrigate extensive rice paddies. Controlling these unruly floodwaters has been a long-term struggle. The southern "basket" is the Mekong River Delta, which is almost four times larger than the Red River Delta. Here, annual flooding deposits rich soil, making the Mekong floodplain one of the most productive rice-growing areas in the world. Vietnam's "bamboo pole" is the slender coastal plain connecting the two deltas.

▲ The leaves of palms growing beside the water are used to build houses.

◀ Barges are the trucks of the waterways.

▶ The city of Hanoi lies in the Red River Delta.

▲ Many families live on boats.

▶ Rivers and canals form a transport network. At Can Tho, boats, laden with goods for sale, provide a large floating market.

▼ In warm climates mangroves thrive in tidal mudflats at the mouth of rivers. Small fish and other water creatures breed among their tangled roots.

▼ Enough rice is grown in the Mekong Delta to feed the whole country and then have some to spare.

NAM TIEN— MARCHING SOUTH

T he first Vietnamese lived in a small northern part of the country's present area. After becoming independent of China in AD 939 the boundaries extended to Quang Binh (see map). By about AD 1010, population numbers had grown so much that the need for more land was pressing. To the north loomed powerful China. To the west were the people of Laos and Cambodia. Vietnam began extending its southern boundary in a policy known as *nam tien*— marching south. This movement continued, until by the end of the eighteenth century (1700s), the country finally reached as far south as it does today.

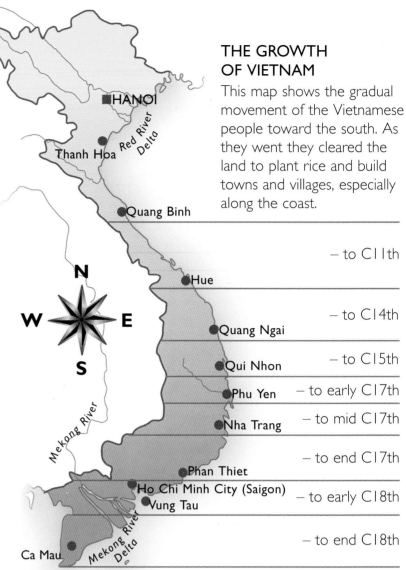

HANOI

Red River Delta

Thanh Hoa

Quang Binh

N

W ● E

S

Hue

Quang Ngai

Qui Nhon

Phu Yen

Nha Trang

Mekong River

Phan Thiet

Ho Chi Minh City (Saigon)

Vung Tau

Mekong River Delta

Ca Mau

THE GROWTH OF VIETNAM

This map shows the gradual movement of the Vietnamese people toward the south. As they went they cleared the land to plant rice and build towns and villages, especially along the coast.

– to C11th

– to C14th

– to C15th

– to early C17th

– to mid C17th

– to end C17th

– to early C18th

– to end C18th

Note: "C" stands for "century"; for example "C11th" = "eleventh century." Pages 14– 21 will show you more about each period (look for the dates at the top of each double-page section).

◀ Students can learn about the history of their country by copying inscriptions dating from the 11th century in the Temple of Literature.

▶ They can also see the remains of Champa in central Vietnam

▼ . . .or visit museums to look at Bronze Age tools.

People on the move take their customs and symbols with them. Images of the dragon, a mythological beast of great importance in Southeast Asian legends, spread throughout Vietnam. This creature represented royalty, power, wealth, and prosperity. The years 1988 and 2000 were dedicated to the dragon in the Chinese and Vietnamese twelve-year zodiac cycle of animals.

▲ The special symbol representing long life traveled from China to Vietnam where it often decorates the doors of temples and pagodas.

▼ A symbol made circular to fit a door.

BASKET MAKING

From earliest times, settlers and travelers have woven bamboo and reeds into containers. Plant material rots quickly in tropical Vietnam, so ancient baskets have not survived. But basketry skills have been passed from one generation to another and continue to thrive. This simple industry has no need for modern machines.

▶ Baskets are remarkably strong and can be used for carrying heavy loads. They are excellent for holding food because they allow air to circulate.

▼ Coracles are basket boats used for fishing in shallow water.

ANCIENT PEOPLES

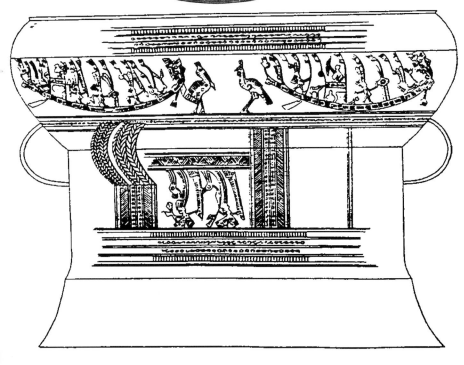

Little evidence survives of the first people who lived in northern Vietnam. From around 400 BC onward, Bronze Age farmers, known as the Dong Son, occupied the Red River valley and coastal regions nearby. Dong Son remains include bronze drums, tools, weapons, and jewelry, and objects of iron and clay. The Dong Son grew rice and kept buffaloes, pigs, and dogs. They believed in the spirits of dead ancestors and in other spirits that controlled the weather and living things. Dong Son drums found in Malaysia and Indonesia show how far these people traded and traveled.

▲ Today, building materials for some houses in Vietnam are the same as they were thousands of years ago.

▲ The Dong Son people engraved their bronze drums with scenes from their daily lives. These pictures of people and animals help to inform us about distant times.

▶ The technique of setting traps in rivers to catch fish has been in use for centuries.

The Viets, who had different customs and a different language from the Chinese, settled in what is now southern China. Groups moved south into the Red River Delta and in 207 BC united to form the kingdom of Nam Viet. The majority of today's Vietnamese are descended from these people.

▲ Modern Vietnamese are descended from those who formed the kingdom of Nam Viet in 207 BC.

▼ The dances of the hill tribes are taught by one generation to another.

HILL TRIBES

About one-tenth of Vietnam's present-day population lives in the highlands. They are the direct descendants of ancient peoples, even though some groups came to this part of the world quite recently. Their lifestyles have changed little through the centuries. Each hill tribe has its own language, customs, and style of clothing. Many still worship the spirits of their ancestors and follow the ancient ways of animism, believing in spirits that protect and spirits that cause harm.

▼ Tassels are woven to give thanks to animist spirits.

▲ ▶ The different hill tribes can be recognized by the fabric patterns of their clothing and the jewelry they wear.

1,000 YEARS OF CHINESE RULE

In 111 BC China successfully invaded Nam Viet and so began more than 1,000 years of Chinese rule. The Chinese brought with them the religions of Buddhism and Taoism (see below) and the teachings of Confucius (see page 39). They introduced better ways of preventing flooding and more efficient farming methods. Wealthier Viet citizens began to copy Chinese ways of speaking, eating, dressing, and writing.

▲ Long ago, junks, looking not much different from modern junks, visited Vietnam. The sails of these ships are divided by bamboo strips and can be pulled to open or close like a fabric window blind.

▲ Chinese calligraphy (see page 39).

◄ The burning of fragrant incense is a daily religious ritual.

BUDDHISM AND TAOISM IN VIETNAM

The Chinese first brought the Buddhist religion to the Red River area around the second century AD. A few hundred years later, Indians took it to the Mekong Delta region. Followers of Buddha learned that they must overcome desire for worldly possessions and pleasure, and seek spiritual perfection (*Nirvana*). The Viets blended the Buddhist religion with belief in their own gods and the spirits of their ancestors.

Taoism (pronounced "Dowism") is based on the teachings of Laotse, the "Old One," who also emphasized the simple life and the harmony between human beings and nature. Taoism has merged with Buddhism in Vietnam.

▲ The Buddhist One Pillar Pagoda in Hanoi, built of wood and resting on a stone pillar, was originally built in AD 1049, shortly after the Chinese were driven from the country. The pagoda is designed in the shape of a lotus blossom, representing purity and rising from a sea of sorrow.

▶ A Buddhist monk and pagoda.

Secretly, however, the Viets always wanted freedom. In AD 39, Trung Trac and Trung Nhi led a revolt and briefly pushed out the Chinese. For two years the Trung sisters ruled Nam Viet jointly until Chinese soldiers again defeated Vietnamese troops. Around AD 150, a woman named Trieu Au led one thousand men against the Chinese. She lost the battle and killed herself. Ly Bon organized another rebellion in AD 543. He, too, failed but is remembered for introducing guerilla warfare—a method of fighting that depends on surprise hit-and-run attacks.

▶ Trieu Au riding into battle on her elephant.

▲ Kites have been popular in Asia since before recorded history and still amuse and fascinate people. They, too, made their way into Vietnam from China.

▼ The ancient *dan tranh* is still heard in Vietnam, though the 16 strings that were once made of silk are now commonly replaced with metal. This instrument from the East Asian zither family is related to the Chinese *cheng*, which originated in the third century BC.

▶ Vietnamese builders learned how to make terracotta roof tiles during the Chinese occupation.

VIETNAMESE EMPERORS

The Vietnamese finally defeated the Chinese in AD 939. They renamed their land Dai Viet. Government continued in the Chinese way, but Vietnamese emperors now took control. Trade with China and Japan expanded. Vietnamese drama and literature flourished. China once more ruled Vietnam for a brief period in the early 1400s. As the Vietnamese pushed south, they also had to fight with Hindu Chams in central Vietnam. Long before, in AD 192, descendants of seagoing Indian traders had founded the Kingdom of Champa in the region of present-day Da Nang, and the Chams remained strong until AD 1471. Later, the Vietnamese triumphed over the Cambodian Khmer Kingdom in the Mekong Delta.

▲ Statue of a mandarin (a high official) at the tomb of Emperor Ming Mang.

▲ Vietnam's collection o Cham sculptures is the finest in the world.

▲ Kublai Khan, China's Mongol Emperor, attacked Dai Viet in AD 1287, but the Vietnamese, using guerrilla tactics, triumphed against his army of 300,000.

▼ Fai Fo's woodcarvers were skilled at translating the brush strokes of poems into mother-of-pearl inlaid in black lacquered wood.

CHINESE MERCHANTS

From the 1500s Chinese merchants developed Fai Fo as a center of trade for South East Asia, China, Japan, and India. The Chinese community lived in clans, each with their own schools, hospitals, temples, assembly halls, and cemeteries. Fai Fo was renamed Hoi An in 1954.

▲ Inside these cool, dark shop-houses, many family treasures are still preserved.

◄ Merchants lived in their warehouses.

In the 1500s and 1600s European traders found Dai Viet split by civil war. It was reunited in AD 1802 when Emperor Gia Long changed Dai Viet's name to Viet Nam and moved its capital to Hue on the Perfume River. The French, wishing to make contacts in this part of the world, supported him.

► A tortoise mosaic in the Forbidden City, which was built for Emperor Gia Long at Hue in 1804.

► The Temple of Literature was built in AD 1070. Thousands of Vietnamese scholars and officials studied there. Examinations were hard. The names of successful candidates were recorded on stone pillars carried on the backs of tortoises, animals believed to represent strength and long life.

◄ Some emperors supervised the building of their tombs during their lifetimes. Emperor Tu Duc (1848–83) died shortly before the French took full control of Vietnam.

WRITING

At first Vietnamese was written in standard Chinese characters. Later a style called *chu nom* was adopted, which was based on Chinese characters.

In the 1600s Alexandre de Rhodes, a French Roman Catholic priest, perfected a script called *quoc ngu,* and in 1910 the French made its use compulsory.

Quoc ngu uses the Roman alphabet with additional accents and signs to suit the consonants, vowels, and tones of Vietnamese, a tonal language with six basic tones of voice. The same word can mean different things, depending on how you say it. For example, *ma* said in different rising or falling tones can mean "ghost," "mother," "but," "grave," "horse," or "rice-seedling."

The Vietnamese alphabet contains more letters than the Roman alphabet but has no "f," "j," "w," or "z." Each syllable is written as a separate word, for example, "Viêt Nam" instead of "Vietnam."

▼ Some *quoc ngu* letters with the marks that show the different sounds for the same letter:

a á à ã

▼ Stories and songs were told through water puppets.

FRENCH COLONIAL RULE

France became increasingly interested in Vietnam's farmland and mineral deposits. In 1858 French soldiers captured Da Nang. Three years later they seized Saigon (Ho Chi Minh City). By 1893 France controlled Vietnam, Laos, and Cambodia, renaming them French Indochina. Vietnam was divided into three parts to weaken its national unity. The French opened coal mines and established plantation crops, such as rubber, tea, tobacco, cotton, and coffee. The Vietnamese were used as cheap labor but were prevented from taking part in government by French laws.

▲ The French introduced crusty bread into Vietnam.

▶ The French introduced coffee into Vietnam. Grown in the highlands, it is now one of the country's major exports. Here, harvested beans are spread out to dry.

▲ Notre Dame Cathedral in Ho Chi Minh City, built between 1877 and 1880, is Vietnam's largest Catholic place of worship. The French missionary, Alexandre de Rhodes, first brought the Roman Catholic faith to Vietnam in the early 1600s.

▼ The French built roads, railways, and many grand buildings in Vietnam, such as the Hotel de Ville in Ho Chi Minh City (see page 26).

During World War II, the Japanese overran Indochina. After their surrender and withdrawal in 1945, communist leader Ho Chi Minh declared Vietnam's independence. This was

unacceptable to the returning French, and fighting broke out between them and Ho's followers. The French were defeated at Dien Bien Phu in May 1954. In July, negotiators for the two sides met in Geneva, Switzerland, to decide the future of Vietnam. They agreed to divide the country on a temporary basis into a communist North Vietnam and a non-communist South Vietnam.

▲ The Cao Dai religion, based on a mixture of major world religions, began in southern Vietnam in the early 1920s. Cao Daists must live simply, always speak truthfully, never envy others' possessions, and avoid killing living creatures.

▲ The French allowed the later Nguyen emperors to rule Vietnam in name only. The last emperor, Bao Dai, died in Paris in 1997 after many years in exile. The tomb of Emperor Khai Dinh, who died in 1925, is guarded by statues of mandarins.

HO CHI MINH (1890 – 1969)

Nguyen Sinh Cung was born in a Vietnamese village. He spent years wandering the world and, while living in Hong Kong in 1930, helped to found the Vietnamese Communist Party. The name by which the world knows him—Ho Chi Minh meaning "he who enlightens"—was given to him after 1941 when he returned to Vietnam for the first time in thirty years. Ho established the League for the Independence of Vietnam, known as the Viet Minh. In 1945, he became the first president of the Democratic Republic of Vietnam in the north and led guerilla fighters against the French and then the Americans.

▲
Ho Chi Minh

◄ Ho Chi Min's house, where he lived on and off for the last eleven years of his life, is preserved as a tourist attraction.

► Ho Chi Min's embalmed body lies in this tomb. in Hanoi.

◀ Villagers fled from their destroyed homes, carrying what they could.

WAR IN VIETNAM

Elections in 1956 might have resolved the problem of reuniting Vietnam, but they never took place. Northern and southern governments could not agree. Ho Chi Minh's plan for making the whole country communist was backed by the Soviet Union, which wanted control of the area. The United States wanted to stop communism spreading through Asia and supported South Vietnam in a war against North Vietnam. Many southerners joined Ho Chi Minh's guerilla fighters, known as the Viet Cong. During the long war, bridges, roads, railway lines, buildings, and ports were destroyed by missiles and heavy war equipment from both the Soviet Union and the United States.

Napalm bombs set villages and crops alight, and chemical spray called Agent Orange killed foliage that might hide the Viet Cong during their surprise attacks.

◀ This watchtower was used when the country was divided into north and south in 1954. Vietnam is not divided now.

▲ Rusted war ammunition is still found in Vietnam. Unmarked mines laid across the countryside kill or cripple anyone who treads on them.

The last Americans withdrew from Vietnam in 1975, leaving the Viet Cong undefeated. Civil war ended when North Vietnamese soldiers entered Saigon in late April 1975 and the South Vietnamese government collapsed. It is estimated that more than three million Vietnamese soldiers and civilians died in the war. Millions more were wounded or left homeless. The United States and its allies suffered heavy casualties, too. Many Americans protested against the United States taking part in this war.

▲ Derelict missiles and war equipment are sad reminders of the war. The Viet Cong reused the airplanes they shot down. Tires became rubber sandals. Pieces of engines were recycled. Metal from plane bodies was melted to make tools, surgical instruments, and other things.

▼ A memorial to the Vietnamese people who died at My Lai village in 1968. Their killing by American soldiers was one terrible result of the war.

▲ This tour guide shows a trapdoor entrance to the tunnels.

THE TUNNELS OF CU CHI

At Cu Chi, northwest of Saigon, the Viet Cong hid in a network of underground rooms and passages, which stretched for more than 125 miles (200 kilometers). The living areas, kitchens, weapons factories, and storage facilities were built one above the other. People lived there for weeks at a time, entering and exiting through concealed trapdoors. Portions of the tunnels have now been enlarged so that western tourists can squeeze through them (see model below).

▲ This shop in Ho Chi Minh City specializes in selling national flags and banners.

COMMUNIST VIETNAM

On 2 July 1976 north and south were officially united as the Socialist Republic of Vietnam (or *Cong Hoa Xa Hoi Chu Nghia Viet Nam* in Vietnamese) with its capital at Hanoi. Saigon was renamed Ho Chi Minh City. The Communist Party faced the urgent, difficult, and expensive task of restoring the country. Nations that had previously provided aid to Vietnam were now unwilling or unable to help. The new government took over farms, businesses, and factories (see page 32). Thousands of southerners, who worked for the former regime, were sent to harsh "reeducation camps" where many died. Fear and uncertainty about their future forced others to leave the country.

▲ Soldiers and police officers inspect activities of every kind.

◀ Those who left immediately after the war and in later years often fled hurriedly in unseaworthy boats. Many died on these journeys. Countries throughout the world, including the United States, Canada, and Australia, offered the "boat people" refugee status.

In 1978 Vietnam invaded Cambodia to overthrow the murderous Pol Pot regime. But Vietnam's invasion of its neighbor angered many nations, especially China. After its withdrawal from Cambodia in 1989, Vietnam's standing with the rest of the world improved. Official links with the United States resumed in July 1995. Many Vietnamese are still very poor, but everyone hopes that continuing peace will bring better times.

▲ This billboard celebrated the twenty-fifth anniversary of the liberation of Hoi An.

◀ Bridging-works on the Mekong at Can Tho in 2000. The bridge platform will be laid on this giant concrete support.

▼ All North Vietnam's bridges and many in the south, including this one in the Mekong Delta, were destroyed during the war.

▲ The war destroyed rails, stations, bridges, tunnels, and switching points on the Hanoi to Ho Chi Minh City railway. After the war, repairs were quickly carried out and new "Reunification Express" trains became a symbol of unity.

▼ Major construction works continue in and around Vietnam's urban centers. These workers are using bamboo scaffolding to repair buildings in Ho Chi Minh City.

THE RETURN OF THE CRANES

Vietnamese people place great importance on signs and omens. For them the Eastern Sarus Crane symbolizes faithfulness, long life, and good luck. This elegant bird lived in the Mekong River Delta for centuries. When Agent Orange effectively wiped out the delta's vegetation, all the cranes disappeared. It was 1985 before one was seen there again, but then their numbers have gradually increased. They are now protected in a special reserve.

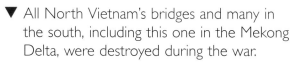

GOVERNMENT TODAY

▲ Vietnam's flag is displayed all over the country.

The Socialist Republic of Vietnam has a National Assembly of about 500 members, which meets twice a year to approve new laws and the appointment of government officials. The Communist Party draws up a list of National Assembly candidates, which is then put to the vote of the people. Elections are held every five years and voting is compulsory for everyone over the age of eighteen. National Assembly members choose the president, prime minister, and a small cabinet of ministers to run the country. Vietnam is divided into provinces and municipalities. People's Committees, also named by the Communist Party and voted for by the people, take care of local government.

► Members of the People's Committee in Ho Chi Minh City meet in the former French Town Hall (Hotel de Ville).

▲ The government looks after Vietnam's roads. Highway One links north and south and carries heavy traffic. This road is in better condition than many others in the country.

▼ Many city buildings have no piped water and so dishes are washed at street outlets.

▲ Postwar engineering projects, such as this irrigation station at Hoi An, have improved water supplies in agricultural districts.

◀ The Presidential Palace in Hanoi was built by the French.

▼ The government controls all the broadcasting stations and newspapers in Vietnam. This means that the people hear only the opinions of those in authority and no one can publicly criticize the government.

▲ The government spends large amounts of money on Vietnam's armed forces. At eighteen years old, a young man must begin two years of military service.

▼ The government funds city sports teams and spectators can watch tournaments free. The most popular sport is *da banh* (soccer). Other favorite sports include volleyball and table tennis. In 2000 businesses sponsored cycle races.

▶ Vietnam's unit of currency is the *dong*. The note of lowest value is worth 200 *dong*. The note of highest value is worth 50,000 *dong*.

◀ National days and parades provide opportunities for waving the flag with pride.

VIETNAM AND THE WORLD

Although Vietnam's history stretches back before recorded time, the country is young in terms of modern industrial methods and computerized systems. The war and the Communist Party's policies immediately after it delayed technological progress and economic growth. The present government welcomes international investment and trades with many other countries in Asia and with western nations. Vietnam belongs to the United Nations (UN), and became a member of the Association of Southeast Asian Nations (ASEAN) in July 1995. Border tensions sometimes arise between Vietnam and its neighbors, especially with China.

▲ There are now more than three million Vietnamese living in other countries. These young people from Australia are part of the worldwide Scouting movement.

WATER PUPPETRY

Water puppetry, or *mua roi nuoc*, is uniquely Vietnamese but puppet troupes also perform outside Vietnam. Water puppetry began in the delta villages around Hanoi at least 1,000 years ago. The brightly painted, wooden puppets representing people, animals, and mythical beasts have movable heads and upper limbs. The puppeteers stand waist deep in water, concealed from the audience behind a slatted bamboo screen. They manipulate the puppets on the end of long poles—up to three poles for some characters.

▶ Musicians, singers, and exploding firecrackers provide lively sounds for the performances.

▼ Vietnam's zookeepers are working with world experts to preserve the country's endangered species. The tiger is one of the most at risk.

▲ Many Vietnamese people now live in other countries. Hoa Trung painted this picture of the Mekong Delta when she was twelve years old and attending St. Monica's Primary School in Footscray, Melbourne. She left Vietnam when she was eight.

▶ Foreign visitors to Vietnam's cities find the cyclo is the speediest method of transport.

▼ Souvenir models are still being made of surplus metal from the war period.

◀ Australia donated 60 million dollars and the Vietnamese government 31 million dollars toward the cost of building the My Thuan Bridge across the Mekong River. It was opened in 2000.

FARMERS AND FISHERS

In a land that is mainly shades of green, the vivid hue of rice plants dominates the countryside. Rice farmers depend on the long monsoon rains and in some places are able to grow two crops a year. Steep hillsides in Vietnam are cut into terraces to provide level ground for farming. Millions of trees have been felled or burned to clear more land. Besides rice, major crops include cassava, sweet potatoes, peanuts, sorghum, and maize. Coffee, tea, and rubber are grown for export as well as sugar cane, soybeans, coconuts, and cashews.

▲
Raising rice is hard work at all stages—planting and transplanting; harvesting; and separating the grains from the straw.

Vietnamese Proverb:

The educated man goes before the farmer. But when the rice begins to run short, the farmer comes first.

▲ Fields of flowers and
► fresh vegetables
ready for the market.

Along the coast people fish for a living, catching lobster, squid, shrimp, and scale fish. Some of the catch is processed in factories and sold overseas. There are also many fish farms in the canals and irrigation channels that supply water to the rice paddies. Some houses built out over water even have enclosures full of fish under their floors.

▲ Large fishing trawlers supply the market, but many catch a meal by casting a fishing net from a river bank or from a boat.

◄ A catch must be sorted quickly before the sun can spoil it.

INDUSTRY AND SMALL BUSINESS

After the Vietnam War, the government set up communal farms and produce was distributed by the state. People were no longer allowed to run their own businesses. This policy was not a success. In 1986 the government introduced *doi moi*, which means "new change." *Doi moi* allowed individuals to control businesses again and to possess land. Since 1986 the county has become richer. Vietnam's factories cluster around Hanoi and Ho Chi Minh City. Many are still owned and run by the government.

▲ ▼

At this refinery in the Mekong Delta sugar canes are turned into sugar grains. Some sugar cane goes straight to the local markets.

◄ Sixteen mattresses can be transported on one bicycle cart!

▲ This poster says: "Da Nang's people commit to build the city to become rich and modern."

◄ Tin cooking pots are turned out in thousands.

► Sport shoes are exported to many countries.

Factories process food and make fertilizers, cement, plastics, bicycles, cotton cloth, shoes, steel, paper, farm machinery, and rubber goods. Vietnam's forests contain valuable hardwoods. The country also has useful deposits of phosphates, tin, zinc, lead, manganese, and gold. Coal and crude oil are among its major exports. Electricity is generated from fast-flowing water and coal-burning power stations.

▲ Salt production is an important industry.

▲ Motorcycles, which are in constant need of fueling and repairing, provide much-needed jobs in towns and cities.

NHÂN DÂN ĐÀ NẴNG QUYẾT TÂM
XÂY DỰNG THÀNH PHỐ GIÀU ĐẸP VĂN MINH

WOMEN AT WORK

Vietnamese women, working in their homes, are experienced weavers of mats and fabrics. Hill tribe textiles feature striking patterns that represent animals, birds, and daily activities, such as pounding rice. Dressmakers, needing little space for their sewing machines, turn out silk and cotton clothing.

Hill tribe textile patterns

Toucan's beak

Rice-pounding

Bird's feathers

▲ Hanoi, the "city of lakes," has Hoan Kiem Lake in its center.

TWO MAIN CITIES

Hanoi (*Ha Noi* in Vietnamese) on the Red River and the much larger Ho Chi Minh City on the Saigon River are Vietnam's major cities. Hanoi serves as the political capital. Ho Chi Minh City is the economic capital and the country's largest port. The cities' centers contain parks, wide streets, and European-style and modern buildings, which are used as universities, colleges, museums, libraries, art galleries, shops, and hotels. In the older districts, streets are narrow and crowded with markets, small shops, and homes. People also live on wooden boats. In both Hanoi and Ho Chi Minh City, street sellers call and sing continuously above the constant noise of traffic.

▲ Houses in Hanoi are built close to one another.

◄ Some city streets are lined with trees.

▼ Motorcycles and bicycles outnumber cars in Ho Chi Minh City by a hundred to one. Some riders cover their noses and mouths to keep out the toxic fumes from sputtering exhaust pipes.

▼ Fashionable boutiques offer clothes for the young and the wealthy.

▲ A main street in Ho Chi Minh City.

▲ The Vietnamese flag in the streets of the capital, Hanoi.

► *Pho Hang Bac*—Silversmith Street. In Hanoi's Old Quarter 36 streets are named after the goods they sell or used to sell.

PHỐ HÀNG BẠC

Old Quarter shops spill their goods on the pavements—birdcages, ceramics, and other things. Flower and food markets open at dawn.

► The Saigon River carries heavy traffic.

▲ Being Vietnamese means taking part in a dragon parade

BEING VIETNAMESE

Vietnamese legend tells of a dragon lord, Lac Long Quan, who married a beautiful fairy princess, called Au Co. Their one hundred sons became the first Vietnamese people, half going with their mother to the mountains and half with their father to the sea. The dragon's favorable links with water and agriculture make it an especially suitable symbol for the Vietnamese. The "children of the dragon," as they sometimes call themselves, have faced invasion, war, typhoons, drought, floods, and famine. Difficult times have made them independent, courageous, hardworking, and, above all, fiercely loyal to their families and nation.

◀ . . .wearing an *ao dai,* a long tunic over trousers. . . and a conical straw hat called a *non la*

▶ . . .or a tasselled cap

▼ . . .or rejoicing in owning a bicycle.

▲ Being Vietnamese means: rising early for *tai chi* exercises on the beach

▲ . . .shopping every morning at the market

▼ Being Vietnamese means visiting an outdoor barber for a haircut

▲ . . .taking part in a game of chance

▲ . . .or mending a punctured bicycle tube.

▲ . . .moving furniture in a motorcycle trailer

▲ . . .or painting in the park.

▶ Being Vietnamese means meeting at the night market for a meal.

FAMILY LIFE

In Vietnamese society, family loyalties are more important than an individual's wishes. Men expect obedience from their wives and children. In return they provide for them as well as they possibly can. Children are seen as the country's future and everyone has time for them. Two to four generations of a family may live together. The Vietnamese respect the elderly and the firstborn son usually takes care of his parents in their old age. Many homes contain a small altar where ancestors are honored. Since the Vietnam War, when so many men were killed, new laws allow women more equality, but they do not have the best jobs or leading government positions.

In Vietnamese names (for example, *Nguyen Bao Quat*) the family name is first, the second may indicate whether the person is male or female, and the third is the given name, by which he or she is known.

◀ *Tet,* the Vietnamese New Year, falls in late January or early February. It is a time for family reunions when the spirits of ancestors are welcomed back. Houses are decorated with branches of pink blossom from the north. Festival food includes strips of melon, candied in sugar, that represent growth and good health.

◀ Transporting three generations—a grandmother rides behind her son with his small daughter in front.

▶ The eldest sister often cares for the younger children while her parents are busy.

◄ Mothers teach their daughters the skills of homemaking and cooking.

CONFUCIANISM IN VIETNAM

The strength of the family unit and the strict social order in Vietnam is based on the teachings and traditions of Confucius, a Chinese thinker. He taught respect for authority figures, such as public leaders, teachers, and fathers. Confucius said that people should "bring comfort to the old, trust in friends, and cherish the young."

▲ A skilled calligrapher helps keep traditions alive for younger generations.

▼ A Vietnamese girl usually lives in her family home until her wedding day. She may have a Buddhist wedding

▲ ...or get married in a western-style white dress.

Housing is limited so many extended families share a small area, such as:

◄ a city apartment;

▼ a house on a platform built out into a river;

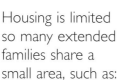

▼ or a house with a very small backyard.

► In the hills, where most people walk everywhere, babies are securely strapped with pieces of cloth to the backs of women or older children.

RICE AND OTHER FOODS

Rice always forms part of a main meal. There are dozens of varieties, each with its own flavor, texture, aroma, and color. Rice is made into noodles, wine, and crunchy edible paper. Other foods include vegetables, fruit, and some fish. Meat is on the menu less often because it is expensive. Poultry, pork, and beef are favorite meats, but snakes, field mice, and other animals are also eaten.

▲ Most country people grow enough food for themselves. Maize is dried before being stored above the living quarters.

◀ Sweet preserved tangerines.

▲ Chopsticks and spoons.

◀ Traditional Vietnamese dishes.

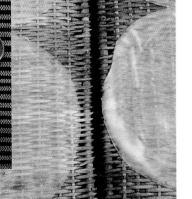

◀ Rice paper is made from puddles of rice gruel dried over a fire fueled by rice husks. Chopped seafood and vegetables wrapped in rice paper become *cha gio* (spring rolls).

▶ Star anise, lemon grass, and chilies are often used to flavor food.

▶ Snakes preserved in rice wine produce a beverage said to be very good medicine.

Vietnam's tasty fish sauce, is made from *nuoc mam*— the liquid drained from salted fish that have been left for months to ferment—mixed with garlic, fresh lime, chili, vinegar, and sugar. *Pho* is beef or chicken noodle soup, flavored with herbs and spices, such as star anise, ginger, and cinnamon. Coriander and lemon grass are other popular herbs used in Vietnamese cooking, which has absorbed Chinese, Indian, and French influences to produce a style all its own. Meals are times to linger with family and friends.

▲ The flavors of Vietnamese cooking depend on the ingredients being bought fresh every day. Food-sellers arrive very early at the markets to set out and prepare their wares. Fruit, for example, may be sold in cut pieces.

▲ Fruit or vegetables are carved into the shape of a lotus flower for table decoration.

▲ Cooked snacks are always available at Vietnam's markets. Food is often wrapped in green banana leaves.

◀ Bread is still baked in the French way and sold hot every morning.

◀ Blocks of ice are delivered to shops and restaurants that do not have refrigerators.

▶ Cooks select the poultry they intend to serve for dinner from a choice of live ducks and chickens.

SCHOOL DAYS

▲ This senior student would hope to attend university to improve her qualifications. She may need to work to support herself or her family.

Education is regarded as very important in Vietnam. Free schooling is available for children from the age of six, but the government cannot afford buildings and teachers for the millions of students. So the school day is divided into two shifts—four hours in the morning for some children, four hours in the afternoon for others. The school year begins in September and runs for nine months, from Mondays to Saturdays. Life in the classroom is strict and children are expected to work very hard. Many leave school after finishing primary grades. Secondary students are eager to pass difficult examinations to admit them to colleges or universities.

▶ The French built many schools, which are still in use. This high school is in Hoi An.

▲ The sound of a gong signals school is about to begin.

▶ High school students often ride bicycles to school but younger children usually walk.

▲ ▼

Final examinations can open the way to university, but when a boy turns eighteen he will spend two years learning to defend his country.

▲ Uniforms are not worn in many small rural schools

◄ . . .but in larger schools uniforms are usually compulsory. These girls are middle primary students.

▶ After school children may purchase a snack

◄ . . .or do their homework with help from father

▼ . . .or work in the family's business—these boys are moving incense sticks

▶ . . .or just wait at a parent's market stall.

▲ Bright patchwork flags tell you that there is a festival nearby.

VISITING VIETNAM

Vietnam is long and so is its history. Rushing about is unwise, unrewarding, and impossible in many places. City streets are usually busy and crossing them requires practice—walk at an even pace, without stopping, so the traffic can weave around you. Traveling anywhere by bus, train, or boat is slow, but there is always much to see on the way. New sights, sounds, smells, and especially tastes crowd the senses—Vietnam is said to have at least 480 traditional dishes. The people have spent the last quarter of a century rebuilding their war-damaged country. They welcome visitors who have time to look and listen.

◄ ► Visitors who manage to reach hill tribe country may see and hear the rhythms of a traditional dance.

Vietnamese Proverb:

If you want to gather a lot of knowledge, act as if you know nothing.

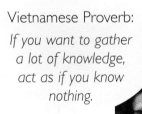

VIETNAMESE CUSTOMS

- Women do not shake hands with each other or with men.
- Touching a person's head is disrespectful because it is believed that this harms the spirit that lives there.
- Pointing your feet at people when seated is thought to be very rude.
- When inviting a friend on an outing, the person who offers the invitation pays the bill.
- Appointment times may not always be kept promptly.

▲ Walk across Hanoi's Huc Bridge

▲ . . .sample the foods of different regions

◀ . . .visit the Temple of Literature in Hanoi

▼ . . .explore the Champa ruins in My Song.

▶ . . .see a junk with tattered sails on Halong Bay

▼ . . .or a beautifully crafted model of a junk in a museum.

▼ Watch a whole shop on a bicycle go by!

INDEX

PICTURE CREDITS
Abbreviations: r = right, l = left,
t = top, c = center, b = below

Mike Langford
Cover; Title; **9** c; **10** tl, bl, br;**12** bl,
bc, br; **13** tl, tr, cl, bl; **15** tr; **16** cl,
cr, bc; **17** tr, br, bl; **18** tr, bl, bc, br;
19 tr, c, bl, br; **20** cl, b; **21** tl, tc, cr,
bl; **22** cr; **23** tl, c, br; **24** tl; **25** tr,
clt, clb, bl; **26** cr, bl; **27** tl, tr, cr, bl,
br; **28** br; **29** br; **30** t, cl, c, bc; **31**
cr, bc, br; **32** tl, bl; **33** cl, crt, crb;
34 tl, cl, bl, br; **35** tl, tr, crt, crb, bc,
br; **36** bl; **37** tl, tc, tr, c, cr, bl, br;
38 bl; **39** tr, cl; **40** tl, trb, cl, c, bl;
41 tl, cl, c, bl, br; **42** tl, cr; **43** tl, cl,
c, cr; **45** tl, tc, cl, cl, cr.

Travel Indochina
Introduction; **8** cl, cr, bl, br; **11** tl,
tr, br; **13** c, br; **15** brt, brb; **16** tl;
20 cr; **21** br; **23** bl; **25** cr; **26** c; **27**
cl; **29** c; **30** t; **31** tl, c, bl; **32** crt, crl;
33 tr, brt, brb; **35** cl, cl, bl; **36** cr;
38 tl, cl; **39** cl, cr, bc; **40** brb; **41** tr;
43 br; **45** tr.
Peter Barker
9 map; **10** map; **12** map; **18** cr; **25** br.
World Expeditions
15 bl; **24** cr; **36** br; **38** br; **44** cl, cr.
**St Monica's Primary School,
Footscray, Victoria**
29 tl, bl; **39** tl, bl; **42** cl; **43** tr, bl.
Denis Buckley
13 cr; **14** cr br; **37** cl; **39** br; **40** trt;
44 bl.

Sue Bliss
11 cl; **26** br; **34** cr; **42** br.
Samsam, Pauline Wesselink
Contents; **22** bl; **32** cl; **43** bc; **45** b.
Belinda Bennett
8 tl, **18** tl
Jane Cameron
26tl, **33** bl (illustrations).
A.A.Balkema Publishers
14 tl
AAP
22 tl
Hoa Tuong
29 tr.
**Maurice Durand Collection of
Vietnamese Art, Yale University**
17 c.

Tony Eardley
15 bc.
**United Nations High
Commissioner for
Refugees**
24 bl.
Vineyard
11 bl; **20** tl; **28** tr; **28** cr,
bl; **32** br; **36** tl; **40** brt,
brc; **44** tl.

Every effort has been made
to consult all relevant
people and organizations.
Any omissions or errors
are unintentional and
should be reported to
Vineyard Freepress Pty Ltd.